BookRags Literature Study Guide

The Man Who Mistook His Wife for a Hat and Other Clinical Tales by Oliver Sacks

Copyright Information

ISBN 978-1-304-52933-6

Table of Contents

Plot Summary

Oliver Sacks is a professor of clinical neurology who has spent years seeing patients. He has compiled some of his more interesting, more personal stories into one volume to share with the world. His goal in writing the book is to present the personal side of neurosis. Often books of this sort are written as a series of case studies full of medical terminology that leaves the average reader frustrated and unwilling to finish the book. Sacks mixes his clinical jargon with a personal empathy for his patients, drawing the reader in and allowing even the most inexperienced reader to gain a better understanding of the lives of the mentally disabled.

Sacks divides his book into four separate but somewhat intertwining parts. Just as many neurological diseases are not mutually exclusive, neither are the stories Sacks compiles. In each section, Sacks highlights several stories of patients suffering from a disease corresponding to the section heading. There are stories of mental losses, mental excesses, mental transports, and the world of the simple.

In the section focusing on losses, the reader is introduced to several interesting people who suffer similar disorders and each cope with their imposed lifestyle in a different way. Dr. P. is able to continue living his life nearly as normally as before the onset of his disease. In fact he is able to adapt his lifestyle to include his disease in a manner that benefits him and his interests. Jimmie G. on the other hand is lost in a world of the past and will never be able to catch up with those around him. For Jimmie G. the world stands still in 1945 and all attempts to bring him up-to-date cause frustration for both him and his doctors. Christina is trying to live a normal life but when she suddenly finds herself without a body she is forced to face herself and her problems. These are just a few of the people the reader finds in Part One and the reader discovers just how quickly and inexplicably a life can change.

Part Two features patients with excesses. Witty Ticcy Ray is possibly the most memorable person from this section. Ray suffers from Tourette's syndrome but suffers is not quite the right word when discussing Ray. Ray has been able to use his syndrome to his advantage in several arenas. He is an excellent drummer because he is prone to lash out into a wild solo and he is wildly entertaining because of his offbeat wit. However, Ray does need some help harnessing his syndrome in order to function reasonably at home and avoid losing his family.

Part Three discusses people with transports. This concept is a little difficult to grasp at first. Although Sacks gives a lengthy description of transports at the start of the section, it is not until the reader reaches the stories of Mrs. O' C. and Bhagawhandi that a glimmer of understanding lights up. Mrs. O' C. hears music in her head--Irish music. The music transports her back to a time in her childhood she thought was lost forever. She is able to warmly remember a mother she barely knew and finds a piece of herself finally restored. Bhagawhandi suffers from an inoperable brain tumor but instead of becoming discouraged that her life will end earlier than it should, she finds comfort in the images that eventually overwhelm her. These images transport Bhagawhandi back to her native India even though she is physically unable to make the trip home.

Part Four is perhaps the most moving and interesting section of the entire book. It is almost sad Sacks chose to leave it until the end, except that if he had placed this section first, the reader might have been disappointed by the lackluster stories of the other three sections. Each story in this section focuses on what Sacks terms "a retardate." These patients are considered "simple" by the medical and social worlds but Sacks brings out their individuality and personal strengths. These stories truly are "stories" and the reader becomes quickly immersed in the lives of these extraordinary patients.

Preface Summary and Analysis

Oliver Sacks explores his reasons for writing his book. He views himself as a type of dual personality--both clinician and romantic. His unique perspective allows him to see the people who are the focus of his case studies rather than merely observe his patients as medical files. Sacks chooses to call his chapters "stories" rather than "studies" and emphasizes that his patients move him to continually work and think. Sacks likens his tales to those of Arabian Nights and asserts that his patients are also heroes and archetypes like those found in fables.

At the outset, the reader becomes convinced Oliver Sacks seeks to present a series of stories, or anecdotes, about some of his more intriguing patients. The reader settles in to be regaled with amusing yet poignant excerpts from the lives of those afflicted with various neurological disorders. However, the reader should note that Sacks is a highly educated man who is readily familiar with Pascal and Nietzsche. These references should caution the reader that such a highly intelligent man may not be able to completely detach himself from the medical world and tell a story in the same vein as a fiction writer. While Sacks hopes to present his "stories" to the reader in a more affable manner than a college textbook, the reader should also be prepared to puzzle through medical terms and philosophical references.

Part One, Losses: Introduction and Chapter One, The Man Who Mistook His Wife for a Hat Summary and Analysis

The introduction to this section discusses the science behind neurological losses and presents some of the history regarding the discovery of diseases. Sacks notes that for a long time popular thought held that the right hemisphere of the brain was regarded as less complex. Thus most disorders of the brain were caused by defects or damage to the left hemisphere. Sacks continues to review his correspondence with several prominent neuropsychologists, including A. R. Luria who advises Sacks to present case histories as stories even if they are just sketches because they prove much more interesting and useful than strict clinical studies. Sacks admits he has become preeminently preoccupied with the representation of self in his patients and this is the focus of most of his stories.

The first story presented is that of Dr. P. Dr. P. is a well-known musician and teacher of music who seems to suddenly develop a problem recognizing the faces of his students. In addition to failing to recognize faces, Dr. P. sees faces on inanimate objects. When Dr. P. comes to Sacks for treatment, Sacks is at first unable to comprehend why the man has been referred to him. However, as their time together lengthens Sacks notices that while Dr. P. looks at him, he does not seem to actually see him. A physical examination reveals the first real oddity--Dr. P. fails to recognize his own shoe and replace it on his foot.

Unable to make a concrete diagnosis, Sacks visits Dr. P. in his home. There he presents a series of pictures, cartoons, and portraits to Dr. P. who is able to recognize most of the items shown. However, Sacks comes to believe that Dr. P. recognizes them only because he fixates on one salient feature which he remembers as belonging to a particular item or person. Dr. P. is a machine able to recall stored information but unable to attach any personal significance to what he sees. Even pictures of close friends and family do not jog evidence of recognition on Dr. P.'s face.

Mrs. P. tells Sacks they must maintain a strict routine or else Dr. P. becomes disoriented. In order to accomplish everyday tasks like dressing or using the bathroom, Dr. P. sings to himself. If the singing is interrupted then Mrs. P. must carefully redirect Dr. P.'s attention until he resumes the singing and the task. A series of paintings hang on the wall, showing Dr. P.'s progression towards his present state. Each picture becomes increasingly devoid of reality. Despite all his difficulties, Dr. P. remains an upbeat and intelligent man. Sacks recommends Dr. P. continue to focus on music and although he never sees Dr. P. again, Sacks learns that he continued to teach music until the end of his life.

Sacks concludes the story of Dr. P. with a postscript that focuses on the lack of science's consideration of judgment. According to Sacks, judgment is a higher faculty that must be considered but is often left out of psychological determinations. In this respect, the science that tries to help patients is as out of touch with reality as Dr. P. Sacks asserts that the failure to place proper emphasis on the patients' judgmental abilities is a disservice to the patient and the science.

Sacks presents an interesting case in Dr. P. The reader is able to imagine a conversation with this intelligent but slightly afflicted man and empathize with his plight. However, just as the reader is becoming engrossed in Dr. P.'s situation, Sacks finishes his tale and gives no explanation why he did not continue contact with Dr. P. The reader wonders if Sacks just dropped the gentleman from his caseload or what possible cause there was for Dr. P. not receiving further evaluation or treatment. Sacks takes the reader to the point of familiarity with the subject of his story but fails to really make the best use of the anecdote as a "story." He is unable to pull himself completely out of the clinical realm and the reader soon becomes lost in medical jargon that is not clearly explained. Just as Sacks complains that the medical profession provides a disservice to patients by not wholly considering them, Sacks does a disservice to the reader by baiting him with a tantalizing tale that is cut abruptly off before the reader is ready to let go of Dr. P.

Part One: Chapter Two, The Lost Mariner Summary and Analysis

A quote by Luis BuÃ±uel begins this chapter about Jimmie G. The quote refers to the loss of memory and the important role memory plays in our lives. Jimmie G. is brought to the Home for Aged where Sacks works. Jimmie is forty-nine years old and is a nice looking and amiable man. On their first meeting, Jimmie tells Sacks all about his life up until his days in the Navy. Sacks leaves the room and when he re-enters, Jimmie starts to recount his tale from the very beginning. Jimmie is shown to have an excellent memory for the past but the present escapes him shortly after it happens. His intelligence is not impaired in the least but he is unable to recall a series of presented objects after they have been hidden from sight for only a few minutes.

Jimmie is stuck in time around 1945. He does not recall events that have happened since this time and is shocked when presented with proof that it is 1975. There appears to be no explanation as to why Jimmie's memory ends at 1945. Testing does not reveal any physical brain damage and the only medical report on Jimmie notes that he suffers from alcohol induced brain damage. A discussion with Jimmie's brother reveals that Jimmie left the Navy in 1965 and since then seemed to be in a downward spiral without the structured lifestyle of the military. However, there is still no explanation why his memory stopped in 1945 and not 1965.

Sacks begins to wonder if Jimmie even has a soul. When questioned, Jimmie reveals that he does not feel miserable but that he does not feel good either; in fact he feels nothing. He is able to engage in simple games but soon feels useless. Sacks then puts Jimmie to work typing but although Jimmie never directly states it, Sacks gets the sense that Jimmie feels this too is just mindless activity. The one place where Sacks sees a glimmer of "self" in Jimmie is at chapel. The chapel and the gardens around the Home seem to transform Jimmie and provide a place where he can feel at peace and somewhat "normal."

The postscript to this chapter involves a discussion of retrograde amnesia. In this type of amnesia, patients suddenly lose part of their memory back to a certain date or time period. In some instances the patient may lose sensual memory. One patient became visually impaired but did not realize it. Some patients with retrograde amnesia can make progress. One patient was able to return home for brief visits with his family but would become hysterical upon returning to the group home where he lived. Jimmie G. was able to find some state of calm when for brief periods he was able to appear "normal" and soulful.

Jimmie G.'s story is in many ways heartbreaking. Here is a very intelligent, good-looking man who has been deprived of his life. He is stuck in a world that lacks progress, contains an unfamiliar family, and does not recognize emotion. The reader feels compassion for Jimmie and wishes there was something more to be done to help this man. Sacks, too, senses that there is something special about Jimmie, and that is why Jimmie's story is told with more warmth and feeling than Dr. P.'s. The reader is slightly relieved to learn that Jimmie does not just fade completely away into oblivion. His life does hold a faint tinge of hope and fulfillment. The reader hopes that for Jimmie, BuÃ±el's quote will never be realized--that Jimmie will never completely be devoid of his memory and therefore his life.

Part One: Chapter Three, The Disembodied Lady Summary and Analysis

Sacks begins the chapter with a brief discussion of proprioception or the sixth sense humans posses that monitors physical movement. His story is then about Christina, a young woman in her late twenties with a good job and two young children. Christina is admitted to the hospital to have gallbladder surgery only to have a dream that she can no longer stand or feel objects in her hands. Doctors try to reassure Christina that this is a normal pre-operative anxiety and that everything is fine. However, Christina begins to suffer from the exact ailments in her dream.

She feels her body is "giving way" and that she is disembodied. Testing shows that Christina has lost her proprioception from head to toe. The cause of this loss is a polyneuritis that affects "the sensory roots of spinal and cranial nerves throughout the neuraxis." Dr. Sacks explains to Christina that the sense of one's body is given by three things working together: vision, balance organs, and proprioception. Christina then decides she must learn to use her eyes in order to compensate for her loss of proprioception.

Eight years pass since Christina first went into the hospital and she still has not regained her proprioception, but she has learned to live a sort of life by means of various accommodations. Christina learns to use her eyes in order to move. She has to concentrate very hard on each body part as she moves it, but eventually this method allows her to regain some motor ability. Christina is been able to return home to her children and maintain her job by working from home. She still feels disembodied, or pithed as she describes it to Dr. Sacks, but is at least fighting against her disease instead of resigning herself to it.

The reader stands in jaw-dropping awe of Christina's story. It is unthinkable that a person could suddenly and inexplicably loose all sense of his or her body. Sacks and Christina's doctors explain the loss of her proprioception as a result of an inflammation, or polyneuritis, but this explanation is too simplistic for the reader to accept. A woman goes in for a routine operation, which Sacks never says whether she actually undergoes, and comes out with a life-changing, debilitating disorder.

Equally amazing to the reader is Christina's response to her condition. Most people would probably bemoan their misfortune, ask to die, or become angry at the world around them and remain so forever. Christina however shows a strength of character most people wish they could possess. One wonders if it is her situation as an apparently single mother that pushes her to seek a solution to her difficulty rather than succumb to it. Her young age may also play a factor in her desire to "overcome" her disease and lead a life as best as she can. Sacks does not explore these personal points of Christina's situation but the reader wonders how exactly one could manage to find even a glimmer of a silver lining in the face of such devastating news.

Part One: Chapter Four, The Man Who Fell out of Bed Summary and Analysis

As a young medical student Sacks is called to evaluate a new patient. The young man is admitted in the morning and seems quite calm and even tempered. Then in the afternoon after being awoken from a nap, the man becomes agitated and angry. Nurses find him sitting on the floor and are unable to calm him enough to return him to bed. When Sacks arrives and begins talking with the man, he discovers the patient views his own leg as that of someone else. In an attempt to throw the foreign leg out of his bed the man has thrown himself onto the floor and now cannot understand how to detach the stranger's leg from his own body. Dr. Sacks points out that the leg is the man's own. The young man is disbelieving but is unable to answer Sacks' question about the whereabouts of his proper leg if this one is indeed not his.

The reader may at first respond to this story with gales of laughter. How absurd that a person should not know his own leg! However, the problem is very real for those who suffer from it and is probably extremely distressing. One cannot imagine what it would be like to not recognize a part of one's own body or, when attempting to discard an unwelcome limb, being unable to rid oneself of something unwanted.

The reader may also be frustrated with Sacks in this short chapter for his lack of explanation. In the previous three chapters, Sacks spends considerable time discussing the neurological or medical reasons proposed for a person's disorder. In this chapter Sacks presents the story of a nameless young man who throws himself out of bed while trying to divest himself of an unfamiliar limb. No explanation for the man's distorted perception is given and no clinical discussion of any sort is offered. It makes the reader wonder why Sacks presents this story in this way. By refusing to name the young man, Sacks takes away the man's personal identity--something he claims he did not want to do in the course of writing this book. It is almost as if this story is thrown in just for laughs, but if so, it reflects poorly on Sacks as an author and a doctor.

Part One: Chapter Five, Hands Summary and Analysis

Sixty year old Madeleine J. is admitted to St. Benedict's Hospital where Dr. Sacks works. She is congenitally blind and suffers from cerebral palsy. Madeleine has never been able to live on her own and has been looked after by her family for her entire life. However, she is as smart as a whip and retains all her sensory capabilities. Her biggest complaint is that her hands are useless "lumps of dough."

Dr. Sacks is unable to understand the cause for Madeleine's affliction. She is able to sense touch and pain but unable to integrate sensation and mobility in her hands. All the necessary components are there for her hands to function properly but still they do not. Taking a cue from Goethe, Sacks decides he must first stimulate an impulse in Madeleine if there is to be the possibility of her gaining the use of her hands. Sacks instructs Madeleine's nurses to leave her food tray slightly out of reach. They are not to deprive the woman of food but to act as if they absently forgot to push the tray as near as usual.

One day, frustrated by the position of the tray, Madeleine reaches out and grasps a bagel. This initial movement leads to a rapid succession of exploring other items around her. Madeleine becomes so excited by the new use of her hands that she takes up sculpting. Madeleine's vast improvement sparks a series of questions in Dr. Sacks about the application of such re-realization of body parts in other patients. Sacks does not explore these questions in depth but merely poses them to himself and to the reader. Madeleine's "recovery" certainly makes one wonder if the possibility exists for other similar recoveries to be made.

Madeleine's story brings up another interesting point: was Madeleine truly unable to utilize her hands due to a neurological deficit or was she merely "babied" for too long, as Sacks speculates? How often do the caretakers of the ill increase the severity of an illness by their over protective care? If Madeleine was never made to feed herself as a young child, then she certainly would not know how as an older woman. The reader should not doubt that Madeleine suffered from a disorder but realize that certain aspects of her disorder could have been exacerbated by the type of care she received early on in life.

Part One: Chapter Six, Phantoms Summary and Analysis

This chapter is comprised of four brief stories that tell about people who suffer from phantoms of differing kinds. The first tells of a sailor who lost his right index finger in an accident. For forty years after the accident, the man constantly worries he will poke himself in the eye simply because the index finger was in the extended position when lost. The man still "feels" his finger is there, fully extended, and will cause further injury if he is not careful about how he touches his face with that hand.

The next anecdote discusses the importance of phantom limbs for amputees. When an amputee receives a prosthesis, it is almost necessary the patient sense a phantom limb in order for the artificial limb to work properly. One patient of Dr. Sacks tells how he must "wake up" his phantom limb each morning before he can properly put on and use his artificial limb.

The third story mentions positional phantoms. Some patients appear to suffer from some sort of balance disorder but upon closer examination are discovered to have visual phantoms. These visual phantoms alter the patient's perception of where the floor or walls are, so that they stumble about as if severely drunk. In most cases, the patient must use their eyes and look directly at an object in order to make it remain still so that they do not stumble about.

The final short section and the postscript to the chapter deal with the possible necessity of phantoms. One patient says his phantom foot can be bad and painful unless he puts on his prosthesis. When the artificial limb is in use, the phantom foot behaves properly and is helpful. Sacks' purpose in this chapter appears to be his desire to promote the notion that phantom limbs and pains are not necessarily bad things for the patient to experience. The reader may notice that Sacks' examples are devoid of any mention of cases where the phantom caused the person more harm than good and so Sacks' argument here may be skewed. However, he does present an interesting idea. Often the memory of a lost limb or pain seems to inhibit the patient from functioning normally after its removal. These stories illustrate that not all patients react the same to similar situations. Like Christina in Chapter Three, these patients have chosen to accept their lost limbs and use the phantoms to their advantage.

Part One: Chapter Seven, On the Level Summary and Analysis

This story is one of the few in the book that is full of personal emotion on Sacks' part. Mr. MacGregor is an extremely likable fellow who is coping exceptionally well with his disorder. In fact he puts his problem to use, in combination with his personal knowledge, and invents a remedy for himself that also helps out several other patients.

At the age of ninety-three Mr. MacGregor is living in St. Dunstan's, a old folks home where Dr. Sacks once worked. He comes to Sacks' office one day complaining that other patients say he tilts to one side when he walks. Sacks videotapes Mr. MacGregor walking and the old man discovers that he does indeed tilt significantly to one side. Mr. MacGregor contemplates what he has just witnessed and determines to find a way to fix his tilt. Once a carpenter, Mr. MacGregor is familiar with different types of levels and devises to construct a level that will help him stay upright.

Together Sacks and Mr. MacGregor work to construct a pair of glasses from which a pendulum is suspended. Mr. MacGregor watches the pendulum and is then able to determine if he is tilting or straight up. At first Mr. MacGregor is exhausted by constantly watching the pendulum but, over time, the process becomes almost second nature. Eventually, almost a third of St. Dunstan's patients are wearing Mr. MacGregor's spectacles.

As already noted, there is a warmth to this story found in few others, such as Chapter Two and Jimmie G. In this story, Dr. Sacks fully succeeds in presenting the individual and not just a patient with a disorder. The reader can fully appreciate Mr. MacGregor and envision the elderly gentleman tilting into Sacks' office. Mr. MacGregor is an extremely likable character and the reader is impressed by the man's outlook on life, in spite of his personal difficulties.

Part One: Chapter Eight, Eyes Right! Summary and Analysis

This chapter is about Mrs. S. Mrs. S. is a woman in her sixties who suffers a massive stroke that affects the right side of her brain. As a result of the stroke Mrs. S. is unable to recognize objects placed to her left. She does not see food on the left side of her tray; she does not put lipstick on the left side of her mouth. In an attempt to remedy this problem Mrs. S. is provided with a rotating wheelchair that she can wheel around to find things on her left. This "fix" increases the amount of food that she eats but does not help her make-up problem. The introduction of a video system only upsets Mrs. S. because to her there is nothing on the left side of her face and so the picture of herself in the monitor is disturbing.

Gone from this short chapter is the warmth found in the previous chapter about Mr. MacGregor. Mrs. S. is nothing more than a case study patient whose story is used to illustrate the possible "cures" doctors can utilize with stroke patients. Sacks notes at the end of the chapter that Mrs. S. refusal of the video system is upsetting to research because doctors were hopeful that such a method would prove productive.

Part One: Chapter Nine, The President's Speech Summary and Analysis

This is perhaps one of the more difficult chapters in the book. The reader is almost required to read the chapter several times before comprehension begins to set in. The subject of the chapter is aphasia or the inability to comprehend words. However, patients with aphasia have an enhanced understanding of the tone with which words are spoken. Sacks spends a great deal of time explaining this phenomenon before getting to the "story" part of the chapter. Perhaps his immediate focus on the clinical rather than the story is what confuses the reader.

The story is relatively short and tells of Emily D. a former English teacher who now suffers from aphasia. Emily must pay close attention to word use and can no longer follow slang speech. As Emily listens to President Reagan's speech she announces that he is "not cogent" because his prose is not spoken properly. Emily shows how the "normal" listener is easily taken in by the preprogrammed speeches of government officials. Emily is able to recognize that the president speaks in loops and turns, while the average listener succumbs to these deceptive devices.

Emily presents an interesting case because she is one of the patients in the book who in many ways does not seem sick. Emily has an ability that most people do not possess and she is able to understand speech better than the average healthy listener. It unfortunate though that Sacks compares Emily, indirectly, to dogs. Dogs, like aphasiacs, are able to sense when a person is being deceptive. This comparison is interesting but certainly not the type of personal remark that one expects to find in Sacks' book. The comment is demeaning and should be re-evaluated. People are certainly not dogs and the reference belittles Sacks' patients.

Part Two, Excesses: Introduction and Chapter Ten, Witty Ticcy Ray Summary and Analysis

Neurology recognizes deficits but fails to acknowledge that sometimes the problem stems from an excess. In neurology, the idea of the brain having too much of something is inconceivable. It seems a paradox to say that something which makes the patient feel extra-healthy is actually a disease.

Witty Ticcy Ray begins with a background discussion of the discovery of Tourette's syndrome. After an initial influx of Tourrette's patients, it seems the disease has all but disappeared. This ia in part due to a facet of the disorder in which patients become slave to a trance-like sleep that can last for years. When Dr. Sacks first encounters patients in this sleepy state, he gives them a dose of L-Dopa. The drug in turn awakens the brains of his sleepy patients and sends them to the opposite extreme--extreme good health accompanied by tics and frenzy.

Ray comes to see Dr. Sacks at the age of twenty-four. He suffers from almost debilitating tics that occur every few seconds. Ray has suffered from these tics since the age of four but, because of his high intelligence, manages to complete college and get married. Ray has been unable to successfully maintain a job because of the severity of his tics and his marriage is threatened due to an increase of derogatory remarks brought on by the excitement of sexual arousal. Ray has so far been able to enjoy success as a jazz drummer where his sudden outbursts on the drums are hailed as brilliant. Ray is also well liked at parties because of his outrageously witty comments.

Sacks starts Ray on a treatment of Haldol which Ray finds frustrating. The drug impairs his balance, speed, and timing so that he is slower than usual, resulting in bruising from being stuck in a revolving door. Ray does not want to live completely free of his tics because they are a part of who he is, but he does want a way to manage them. Sacks then prescribes a treatment period of three months during which time he and Ray will thoroughly explore all aspects of Tourette's and life without tics. After three months, the inclusion of Haldol will be readdressed.

The complete understanding of his disease coupled with the drug treatment enables Ray to lead a tic free life without feeling he has lost part of himself. Ray further refines his treatment so that during the week he takes Haldol as prescribed and is a model husband, father, and employee. On the weekends he decreases his Haldol dose so he is still able to enjoy his life as Witty Ticcy Ray.

Sacks spends an inordinate amount of time in the introduction and the beginning of this chapter discussing the history of Tourette's and neurology's failure to acknowledge of excesses. The reader wonders if he will ever get to hear about Witty Ticcy Ray. While the medical information is helpful, the average reader gains a better understanding from reading the case story than from pages of clinical jargon.

Ray is an interesting man because he has embraced his disorder. Perhaps this is because he knows no other way of life. Ray continues to accept and even desire his disorder after a "remedy" has been found. Ray is an example of how a disorder can in some ways enhance a patient's life. If not for his Tourette's, Ray might not have enjoyed a side career as a jazz drummer. This aspect of his life is enhanced by his Tourette's, not hampered by it. What is also interesting about this chapter is the way Sacks works with Ray to treat the disease. The first round of treatment is solely doctor directed, but when patient and doctor work together a much more agreeable solution is discovered. Patients should be consulted in the management of their disease. After all, who knows a disorder better than those living with it?

Part Two: Chapter Eleven, Cupid's Disease Summary and Analysis

At the age of eighty-eight, Natasha K. is suddenly overcome by a feeling of extreme well-being and flirtiness. She self-diagnosis herself with Cupid's Disease, or syphilis. In her younger years Natasha worked in a brothel and feels that she could have caught the disease then but it has lain dormant all these years. A test of her spinal fluid reveals she is correct. When the subject of treatment is broached, Natasha is a little uncertain. She is enjoying her new found freedom but does not want the disease to progress further. A course of penicillin is prescribed to kill the spirochetes which spread the disease, but there is nothing that can be done to reverse her cerebral changes. So Natasha will be able to continue living her flirty lifestyle.

In the postscript to this chapter, Sacks discusses another patient who would draw a more detailed picture than the one presented him. Each time Miguel becomes excited by the vision he sees in his head and tries to convey that on paper. A dose of Haldol quiets Miguel down to the point where he dutifully copies the original without adding any of his own vision. Sacks realizes a paradox is working here. People live normal lives only to suddenly be awakened to an excited state of excess. Often these patients enjoy their new lifestyle and are reluctant to have it treated. In these cases the illness has made them healthy. What is a practioner to do under these circumstances?

The idea that not all disease is bad or harmful is rampant throughout Sacks' book. Even in the deficits section, the reader sees cases of patients who benefit from their disease. Natasha's case is rather simple in diagnosis and treatment. She enjoys her new life and, at the age of almost ninety, who can blame her for wanting to maintain this increased level of excitement? Again the reader sees doctor and patient working cooperatively to arrive at a treatment beneficial to the patient. Natasha is able to remain flirtatious but without risking her physical well-being. The reader wonders if Sacks is in the early stages of his practice or the later stages. It would be interesting to read these stories in chronological order and see if Sacks learns to work with his patients only after several years, or if he is just a young medical student eager to embrace the field.

Part Two: Chapter Twelve, A Matter of Identity Summary and Analysis

Dr. Sacks walks into a room to meet with William. When William sees Sacks, he identifies him first as a customer in the deli William used to operate, then as an old friend, then as Hymie the butcher next door, and finally as a doctor. The progression from one identity to the next is rapid fire, but the result is that William becomes scared at his inability to correctly identify who he is with and where he is. As soon as correct recognition begins to take hold, William begins the series all over again, assuming once more that Sacks is a customer in his deli.

William Thompson suffers from Korsakov's but does not realize it. He dances from one fantasy to the next with the ability to make those around him believe he is perfectly normal. He has even managed to leave the hospital and take a taxi ride. For the duration of the ride, the driver believes that William is a reverend. William has only recently been diagnosed with Korsakov's and is still suffering from the initial delirium of the disease.

The reason William tells such fanciful stories is because that is what he perceives that each person does in order to identify himself. Every person has a story we tell people about ourselves in order to distinguish ourselves from one another. William no longer remembers his own story and so he must invent new stories for himself. This state of mind is rather sad because William's stories are false; he has no sense of reality. On a rare occasion he does, as when his younger brother walks past a window and William correctly identifies him. At the same time, William asserts that his older brother is still alive and states, when told that his brother died almost twenty years ago, that "George is always the joker!" In this sense, William is not like Jimmie G. discussed in Chapter Two. William is forced to live a long unending fantasy from which he cannot be rescued. Jimmie G. was able to be found on occasion and revisit reality for short periods of time. The only time William finds a modicum of relief is when he ventures out into the gardens alone, where he is not continually forced to invent new stories and can relax.

The reader may find William's story to be one of the saddest in the book. While William is interesting and funny because of his invented stories, the reader soon realizes that this is life for William. William will not remember his brother George died or any other significant detail of his own life. William does not know who he is and so lives in a fantasy world he must constantly make up. This is an exhausting existence. To be forever trapped in a world of fantasy is something a child would find fun, but for an adult it is a prison sentence with no release date.

Part Two: Chapter Thirteen, Yes, Father-Sister Summary and Analysis

Mrs. B used to be a research chemist, now she suffers from a change in personality. When Dr. Sacks enters the room she rapidly addresses him as Father, Sister, and Doctor. Mrs. B. sees parts of people, not the whole person. Sacks' beard reminds her of a priest, his white coat of a nun, and his stethoscope of a doctor. So to Mrs. B., Sacks is all three people. Mrs. B does not have a problem with this way of perceiving her environment and does not understand why Sacks makes a fuss over it.

In the postscript, Sacks notes that Mrs. B. is not an unusual case. This form of schizophrenia is not uncommon but is puzzling to those close to the patient, including doctors. The patient acts as if he is in a constant state of jovialness but indeed he has lost the center of his world. The patient has no grasp of boundaries with which to ground himself and is left to bounce happily around.

Mrs. B. is quite comical and in some ways the reader may agree with her perception of the world. What do titles matter? Is it important that Mrs. B. acknowledge Sacks as a doctor and not a Father or Sister? As long as Mrs. B. has found a way to function and is not noticeably bothered by her disease then what harm is there in letting her address people as Father-Sister or Sister-Doctor? The story of Mrs. B. points out the difficulties encountered not by patients but by their loved ones. Sacks does not spend a great deal of time talking about the effect Mrs. B.'s new personality has on others. While Mrs. B. is content, it is the people around her who are grounded in reality that have trouble accepting and coping with her disorder. Therein may be one of the central problems of mental health: the afflicted manage in their new lives, but the healthy become the afflicted because there is no treatment for lack of understanding.

Part Two: Chapter Fourteen, The Possessed Summary and Analysis

Sacks returns to Tourette's Syndrome by re-directing the reader's attention towards the severer forms of the disease. Witty Ticcy Ray was a relatively mild case of the disorder when compared with the complete possession some patients experience. Sacks notes that once he had his first encounter with Ray, he began to see people with Tourette's everywhere. According to Sacks, James Parkinson identified Parkinsonism while walking the streets of London, not sitting in a lab or hospital.

Shortly after meeting Ray, Sacks is walking down the streets of New York when he witnesses a woman imitating passers-by. Her characterizations become increasingly unacceptable to those around her until a large disturbance occurs. As Sacks watches he realizes that the woman is not doing this act on purpose but is being possessed by her Tourette's. She has no other choice but to momentarily adopt the mannerisms of those she passes. As the people around her become increasingly upset, so too does the woman. Her mannerisms increase according to the responses of the passers-by. Just as it seems that neither the woman nor the crowd will be able to handle anymore of her antics, the woman ducks into an alley where she appears to become ill as if expelling the amassed identities from herself.

Sacks learns more about Tourette's in that one episode on the street than in a thousand lab hours. He realizes that patients with Tourette's are aware of their disorder and must constantly wrestle with taming or living with the disease. The Tourette's patient is forever overcome with uncontrollable impulses. He cannot will away these impulses or repress them but must succumb to them as they take over. The question then becomes where is the self in all of this chaos? Sacks brings up the question of what is happening to the possessed woman during her possession. It is an interesting thought. Where does the real woman go? Is she still there, under layers, trying to fight the impulse to imitate each and every passerby? The reader realizes the enormity of Tourette's in this horrendous moment. At first, the thought of someone imitating each streetwalker in an exaggerated performance is funny. Then the reader realizes this is not a performance. The patient has no control over her actions but must wait for the crowd to thin out or an exit to present itself. The reader wonders how the woman conducts her daily life. Can she hold a job? How does she go to the grocery store? Does this happen around her own family? The list of questions is long and the reader begins to feel truly sorry for the woman. Sacks answers none of these questions either. He appears as befuddled as the reader, but at least the reader is now aware that such situations exist and may have more compassion when walking the streets of their own town.

Part Three, Transports: Introduction and Chapter Fifteen, Reminiscence Summary and Analysis

Sacks describes the patients in this section as suffering from reminiscence or, as he prefers to call it, transports. These patients have a very strong, personal connection to some memory recalled from their deep past and are therefore "transported" to another place or time. Often when a patient suffers from a transport, he does not confess the problem to his medical doctor because he feels the problem must stem from a purely psychological root. However, Sacks is quick to point out that often transports are the result of a physical problem and runs through the underlying physical cause of each of the transports in the section.

The first chapter in this section is quite long compared to the other four and focuses on two elderly ladies, Mrs. O'C. and Mrs. O'M, who each suffer from an auditory reminiscence. Mrs. O'C., who is partly deaf, lives in an old people's home and wakes in the middle of the night after dreaming about her childhood in Ireland. In her awakened state she hears, very loudly and clearly, Irish songs from her childhood. After determining that a radio has not been left playing, she talks with her otologist and then a psychiatrist before being referred to Dr. Sacks. Sacks decides to perform an EEG on Mrs. O'C. but is prevented for sometime due to scheduling. When an EEG is finally conducted, Mrs. O'C. is experiencing the songs to a lesser degree but the EEG still shows increased activity in her temporal lobes. After some time, the songs disappear completely and Mrs. O'C. is slightly sad to have the music turned off.

Sometime later, Mrs. O'M. comes to live at the same home. Mrs. O'M. is also slightly deaf but begins to hear music and indistinct voices. Unlike Mrs. O'C., Mrs. O'M. does not like hearing the music and in fact disdains the three hymns which play continually in her mind. Also unlike Mrs. O'C., Mrs. O'M.'s songs increase instead of dissolving after only a few weeks. For four years she suffers the music in her head before even mentioning the phenomenon to anyone. An EEG reveals a large amount of temporal lobe activity but does not help discover a cause for the musical transport.

The best attempts at explaining this strange phenomenon come from William Penfield who describes these "musical epileptic" seizures as a kind of mental diplopia. The patient is at once suffering from a remembrance of the past and yet still functioning in the present. Sacks spends several pages exploring the meaning of these phrases and Penfield's research, but the reader easily becomes slightly lost. What the reader can take away is that this "disorder" is related to epilepsy in a sense. The music heard by the patients is like a seizure, and indeed for Mrs. O'M., anti-convulsion medicine removes her musical transport.

What is most interesting about these two women is that each reacts so differently to a similar disorder. For Mrs. O'C. the music was a pleasant occurrence because it brought forth memories she never realized she possessed. She was orphaned at a very young age and brought to America and so did not recall much about her own mother. Her musical transport brings a feeling of warmth usually inspired by a parent. Mrs. O'C.'s transport helps to restore her memories of her mother. Mrs. O'M., on the other hand, does not find anything pleasant about the music in her head. She views the transport as a sign she is mad and lives in a state of constant worry before finally seeking help. Mrs. O'M. is never able to discover where these particular songs originate from in her past and feels only revulsion at their presence.

Each woman experiences the same disorder in a completely different manner. For Mrs. O'C. the "disease" brings comfort and makes her feel more complete. When the music ceases to play in her mind, she misses hearing it. The music transports her to a time long locked away. In her old age the music transports her back to a forgotten childhood. The reader may feel the music helps to complete Mrs. O'C.'s life and that when she dies, she will be able to without any lingering regrets over not being able to recall her mother. The musical epilepsy provides a sort of closure, a beneficial function, for Mrs. O'C. On the other hand, Mrs. O'M. views her musical epilepsy as a sign of madness and is ashamed to admit her problem. She is also unable, or the reader may feel unwilling, to discover the root of the songs she hears. Perhaps Mrs. O'M. feels such revulsion at the music in her mind because it transports her to an unpleasant recollection in her memory she does not care to voice. Either way, the cases of these women are fascinating and the reader is struck by how "helpful" some mental disorders can be. One is often repulsed by the words "mental disorder" and does all one can to steer clear of anything involving the mental health field. Mrs. O'C.'s story shows that mental disease is not always repulsive and can in fact increase the state of one's mental health.

Part Three: Chapter Sixteen, Incontinent Nostalgia Summary and Analysis

Sacks takes a brief moment to tell the story of Rose R. Rose is a post-encephalitic patient who suffers reminiscence after receiving L-Dopa treatment. Sacks notes that patients receiving L-Dopa often experience reminiscence. Rose has been in a type of trance for the last twenty-four years due to Parkinsonism. When given L-Dopa, she slowly begins to wake up. At first she begins to recover speech and psychomotor functioning. Rose then begins experience an increase libido which makes her take great delight in smutty stories and jokes. Rose is surprised to discover that she still recalls such things after forty years. Sacks reports that research shows it is often common for a single note of a song or, more commonly, a smell to prompt a recollection of long buried memories. These memories then come flooding back much to the patient's surprise.

This chapter is extremely brief, especially in comparison with the previous one. The story of Rose seems to serve only to reiterate what Sacks has just presented in the story of Mrs. O'C. and Mrs. O'M. The resurgence of memories due to L-Dopa treatment seems to be a clinical fact Sacks desires to place in his book but cannot find a better way to present, so he sticks in a very short story to illustrate the point. The reader is not able to connect to Rose in this brief description and is only slightly amused at the fact that her memories are "dirty" ones.

Part Three: Chapter Seventeen, A Passage to India Summary and Analysis

At the age of seven a sizable tumor is discovered in Bhagawhandi's brain. The tumor is removed and for the next ten years Bhagawhandi lives a full and normal life. Then, at the age of eighteen, the tumor is rediscovered. At nineteen Bhagawhandi is admitted to the hospice where Dr. Sacks works.

At first Bhagawhandi remains in relatively good humor and seems to accept her fate. However, as her tumor grows she begins to suffer from severe and strange seizures. These new seizures are characterized by a dreamy state in which Bhagawhandi sees visions of her native India. Bhagawhandi is not bothered by these visions but instead finds them comforting. At first Sacks thinks Bhagawhandi is suffering from a steroid psychosis, but her visions lack the disorganization associated with steroid induced dreams. As the weeks pass, Bhagawhandi's dreams become increasingly more frequent until she seems to be lost in them completely. The medical staff is hesitant to disrupt Bhagawhandi during her visions. On one occasion Sacks asks what is happening. Bhagawhandi replies she is journeying home. A week and a half later, Bhagawhandi passes quietly away with a faint smile on her face.

Bhagawhandi's story is beautiful and heartbreaking. The reader may feel that all people should be so lucky as to pass quietly away, enveloped in pleasant memories from their life. Of course the heartrending parts of the story is that Bhagawhandi is prevented by her illness from physically returning to India and that she dies at such a young age. It is interesting that the medical staff struggle to find a cause for Bhagawhandi's visions. She is not bothered by them and they pose no further physical threat to her condition; so why do these doctors insist on finding a cause and a cure? It is not until the very final stage of Bhagawhandi's decline that Sacks seems to understand what the reader may have realized much earlier: that Bhagawhandi's visions are a blessing sent to gently convey her "home" and reduce the pain and suffering caused by her tumor.

Part Three: Chapter Eighteen, The Dog Beneath the Skin Summary and Analysis

Stephen D. is a young medical student who engages in drug use, namely cocaine and PCP. One night he dreams he is a dog and is able to "view" the world as a dog would through a keen sense of smell. For three weeks, Stephen is able to smell things he never would have noticed before. He states things are not really real to him until he has smelled them. After his enhanced sense of smell dissipates, Stephen is both relieved and saddened. He feels he loses something generally lost to civilized society.

The thing Stephen loses when his enhanced sense of smell vanishes is a lack of inhibition. Dogs are not inhibited by social standards and so are able to gain a stronger sense of the world around them. However, as Sacks goes on to discuss, humans need a certain degree of inhibition or we would be no more than animals. While the ability to have increased senses can at times by beneficial, lack of inhibition is akin to animalistic behavior.

What is most shocking about this story is that it is considered to be a case of a short-lived mental disorder. Stephen D. admitteds drug use despite being a medical student. The reader should see some red flags here, especially when Sacks reports that Dr. D. is now a successful internist. The reader wonders how a medical student is granted a license to practice medicine after engaging in illicit drug use. Stephen's curious enhanced sense of smell is not particularly worrisome but the medical ethics of his story are. The reader wonders what Sacks' purpose was in including this story. Whatever Sacks' intentions, the reader does not readily grasp them and instead is appalled that a medical student is not reprimanded for using illegal drugs.

Part Three: Chapter Nineteen, Murder Summary and Analysis

Donald kills his girlfriend while under the influence of PCP and then immediately suffers from amnesia and is unable to recall the event. During the trial, the details of the case are not openly discussed in front of the court or Donald because of their horrendous nature. It is concluded that Donald suffered a temporal lobe or psychomotor seizure and is not held responsible for his actions. As "punishment," Donald is committed to an institution.

During his stay in the mental institution, Donald takes up gardening. He is a calm and well-mannered patient and in his fifth year is permitted to take day trips into town. On one such excursion he is riding his bike down hill when he is in an accident that leaves him in a coma. While comatose, Donald makes disturbing outbursts and upon awakening is able to recall the minutest detail of his girlfriend's murder. Donald is submitted to a battery of evaluations and tests to discover the cause of his miraculous recovered memory. However, to this day, no conclusion has ever been reached but Donald has been able to overcome the terror associated with his memories, and although not repressing them, has been able to resume a basically normal lifestyle.

Like Chapter Eighteen, the reader is struck by the supposition that the patient's actions are a result of some mental disorder when both patients, Stephen and Donald, admittedly used drugs at the time of the onset of their disorders. At different points throughout the book, the reader has been confronted by the possibility that a patient's disorder is not really a disorder at all. Madeline J. and her new flirtatious personality are the result of a physical disease, syphilis. Here the cause for the disturbance in Donald's life is of his own doing. Donald used drugs and, in a drug-altered state, murdered his girlfriend. Donald's story begs the long-standing question of who is responsible when drugs or an altered mental state are involved in a crime. Unfortunately, like the reason for Donald's returned memory, there is no clear cut answer.

Part Three: Chapter Twenty, The Visions of Hildegard Summary and Analysis

Like several of the chapters in this section, this one makes little sense. Every story up until this point has been about one of Dr. Sacks's acquaintances or personal patients. Hildegard of Bingen lived in the 1100's and could not have possibly been a patient of Sacks. So what purpose does the inclusion of her story serve? Hildegard of Bingen was an extraordinarily intelligent nun and mystic. She had numerous visions which she recorded and discussed in numerous books.

Sacks does not discuss Hildegard in terms of mental disease or defect. He only mentions the basics about her. The chapter is devoid of medical consideration of Hildegard's "disease" and indeed Sacks does not conclude that she suffered from any disorder. He does provide ample examples of her drawings but there is little discussion about their significance in relation to transports or the other stories in this section. In short, the reader is confused by Hildegard's inclusion and Sacks does little to clarify his intentions in including her in his book.

Part Four, The World of the Simple: Introduction and Chapter Twenty-One, Rebecca Summary and Analysis

Sacks notes he is slightly apprehensive about working with retardates because he thinks the work will be "dismal." He even writes a letter to this effect to Luria who has worked with retardates for some time. Luria's surprising response is that this population presents some of his most rewarding work. Sacks soon finds that what Luria means is that even though these patients are considered mentally defective, they almost always possess a certain endearing characteristic or ability that more than makes up for anything they may lack. Indeed the reader's mind may conjure up images of patients sitting for hours in a chair facing a window while a string of drool drips from their mouth. The mental picture created by the words "mentally slow" or "simple minded" is one provided to us by television, but Sacks changes that picture. This section is perhaps the most heartfelt and interesting of the entire book.

Rebecca comes to the clinic at the age of nineteen after having been referred by her Grandmother. Rebecca is very childlike. She is unable to distinguish right from left or put a key in a door. Rebecca's physical features--a cleft palate, stumpy fingers, thick glasses--make her the target of jokes. However, Rebecca forms lasting quality relationships with people. Her grandmother, who raised her from the age of three, is her closest friend and their relationship is extremely close. Rebecca also has a fondness for stories and poetry even though she herself cannot read them. She delights in the ritual and sanctity of religious activities.

Rebecca often sits and takes in the environment around her. When approached by someone she trusts, she tries to convey to them her wonder and appreciation of the scene before her using constructed bits of poetry. Sacks likens her to "an idiot Ecclesiastes," the poet writer of the Bible. Formal testing frustrates and upsets Rebecca and provides no real indication of her abilities. Sacks notes that when he meets Rebecca, he realizes how inept psychological testing can be since it only reveals deficits not strengths.

When Rebecca's Grandmother passes away, Rebecca handles the situation with remarkable composure. She expresses her grief in an almost lyrical manner and becomes rapt in the process of sitting shiva and holding the position of bereaved. In an attempt to distract Rebecca, the staff enrolls her in a series of classes at the hospital. After a time Rebecca becomes upset with the classes and tells Sacks that she does not want to participate in them any longer. To her the classes do nothing to "bring her together" and she prefers to continue on in her own way. She asks instead to be allowed to participate in theatre, where she excels. Sacks notes in his postscript that one would not think of Rebecca as a retardate if they could see her on stage.

As Sacks mentions in his introduction, the simplest patients are often the most rewarding. Rebecca shows the reader that the world is too hectic, too encumbered by things we should do that we often miss the things we love and want to do. When Rebecca is forced to partake of the clinic classes she becomes less of herself. While the doctor's way of thinking is that the classes offer structure to a seemingly unstructured population, they fail to realize that these patients have a structure all their own. Classes often confront them with their own inabilities and do little more than frustrate them. Left to their own devices, patients like Rebecca are often able to find a niche of comfort where they excel beyond the imagination of any medical practioner.

Part Four: Chapter Twenty-Two, A Walking Grove Summary and Analysis

Martin is admitted to the Home at the age of 61 after being diagnosed with Parkinsonism and is no longer able to care for himself. His father was a famous singer at the Met and Martin grew up exposed to and immersed in a world of music. Following the deaths of his parents, Martin tries to care for himself but his slowness prevents him from keeping a job for any length of time. Throughout everything, he maintains an amazing memory for music.

Sacks wonders if Martin might have also been a famous singer if not for his mental retardation. Martin himself is saddened by his inability to take to the stage like his father but focuses more on his own abilities. He consults on musicals and for churches, staging large musical productions. Martin has sung at the Met and with several choirs in large churches, but always as part of the choir because his tone deafness prevents him from singing solo. As a child, Martin's father would read to him from Grove's Dictionary of Music and Musicians; a tome which Martin has committed to memory. Despite all these accomplishments, Martin is extremely childish. At the home he steadily becomes shunned by other patients and seems to undergo a regression.

When Dr. Sacks confronts Martin about his decreased mood, Martin says he must sing and worship. Sacks immediately makes plans for Martin to attend a church close to the Home where Martin is readily accepted and becomes part of the choir. Soon after his return to singing and church, Martin becomes himself again.

The reader may be mystified that the medical staff was unable to correctly identify the cause of Martin's discontent. They were well aware of his musical background and his strong identification with music, but somehow they were unable to realize that in the Home he lacked this interaction. As in the case of Rebecca, it seems the medical staff feels they are doing a service to the patient by enrolling him in classes or occupying him in "prescribed" activities. It is continually astounding to the reader how poorly Sacks represents the medical staff.

Perhaps he is unable to realize this because his profession calls for him to do the best he can. Maybe only the uninitiated reader has the ability to stand at a distance and see that the doctors and nurses who care for mental patients often miss their mark because they are too consumed with what the textbooks prescribe, instead of listening to their patients. Perhaps this is a function of working in mental health. It is automatically assumed the patient cannot comprehend their situation or speak intelligently about their own care and so the medical staff does what is always done. This seems to be a failure of the entire medical--the patient is rarely treated while the disease receives all the attention.

Part Four: Chapter Twenty-Three, The Twins Summary and Analysis

John and Michael are twins who have been in and out of various institutions since the age of seven. Dr. Sacks meets them in 1966 when they are twenty-six years old. The twins are semi-famous, having appeared on radio and television shows to showcase their savant-like ability to "say at once on what day of the week a date far in the past or future would fall." Interest in the twins begins to wane but Sacks continues to enjoy "studying" the twins in a more laidback manner.

The twins have been subjected to numerous tests in order to understand their unusual ability. They have become a carnival sideshow for people wanting to play with their ability to calculate the date of Easter for the next 80,000 years. As outstanding as this ability is, the twins score appalling low on IQ tests and are unable to solve even simple addition equations. Not only can the twins report on dates in the past and the future but they are able to tell the weather, what they ate, or what they wore on any particular day from their own lives since the age of four. What amazes Sacks is the amount of information the twins can retain. There is seemingly no good explanation for their ability; only that, according to them, they see the information in their minds.

Sacks is baffled by the twins' ability but continues to enjoy working with the pair. One day he encounters them sitting quietly in a corner playing a sort of game together. One twin will say a number and then the other twin will say another number. Not able to immediately recognize the significance of these numbers, Sacks waits until he goes home and then pours through math books and tables until he discovers that all the numbers the twins spoke are prime numbers. Excited by his discovery, Sacks takes one of his books with him the next day and quietly joins in the twins' game. However, when the twins start spouting numbers twelve digits long, Sacks must quit the game because his book does not go past ten digit numbers.

Ten years after his encounter with the twins, Sacks learns that another doctor decided to separate John and Michael. Each lives in a separate halfway house and maintains a menial job. Each twin has done well in his new life but there is something lacking in their demeanor now that they have been robbed of their ability to "talk" to one another in their number speech. Disengaged from one another, the twins no longer have their mysterious numerical ability but this is considered a small price to pay in order to be a functional member of society.

Sacks' post-script to this chapter contains a discussion of algorithims the twins may have used to calculate the dates on a calendar so far in the future. The discussion is interesting but detracts from the reader's connection to the twins. At one point in the story Sacks refers to the twins as "calendar calculators." This is such a sad statement because it reduces the pair to nothing more than a mindless parlor trick. By trying to parse out the means that allows the twins to state dates in the past or future, doctors and researchers remove the human element from the brothers. John and Michael serve as a novelty to be examined but to what purpose? The reader wonders what benefit is being served by discovering the method behind the twins' ability. Since the occurrence of savants is relatively rare, and it is not a life threatening disorder, there seems to be no pressing need to discover the cause of such a phenomenon. Similar to the separation of the twins, the purpose of exhaustive research on John and Michael is purely motivated by idle curiosity and does not seem to benefit the twins.

Part Four: Chapter Twenty-Four, The Autist Artist Summary and Analysis

At twenty-one JosÃ© is labeled an idiot. However, what most people do not know about JosÃ©, because they do not take the time to get to know him, is that he is a gifted artist. Dr. Sacks takes the time to engage JosÃ© in his favorite pastime and even gains an appreciation for the young man's gift.

JosÃ©'s drawings are not exceptionally exquisite but he manages to draw out the feeling of an object so that his interpretation of the original becomes somehow more profound. A watch is no longer a simple watch but has detail the ordinary observer probably would not notice. Sacks has JosÃ© sketch a number of different pictures and is continually amazed at the "fairy tale" quality JosÃ© brings to his renditions. Sacks spends hours pouring over JosÃ©'s numerous charts, trying to discover what has happened to this young man. JosÃ© suffered a very high fever as a child, followed by the onset of seizures, and lost his ability to talk. JosÃ© did retain the ability to draw--a trait his father and an older brother also possess. For a period of fifteen years there is little information regarding JosÃ©'s mental state and his records do not resume until he is admitted to an institution because of a severe outburst of violence.

JosÃ©'s drawings begin to change as Sacks spends more and more time letting the young man express himself. JosÃ© begins to add more detail to the simple pictures Sacks presents him with to copy, as if he is trying to convey something through his pictures that he cannot express in words. Then JosÃ© begins to speak. Although it is very rudimentary and garbled, he attempts speech and the doctors feel this is a good sign. JosÃ© is also moved to a quieter ward where there is less frightening stimuli.

The postscript to this final chapter is perhaps the most moving and Sacks asks the question that should be the focus of all research: is there a place in society for people like JosÃ©? For the majority of patients Sacks discusses throughout his book, there is the opportunity for each one to hold a functional role in society. Each patient is not necessarily in need of a "cure" but in need of understanding and assistance maintaining the life they have been given. Dr. P. is able to continue teaching despite his disorder, Mr. MacGregor uses his disability to create a new type of eyeglasses, Rebecca performs in the theatre, and JosÃ© should be able to engage his creative side in a meaningful manner.

Over and over again the reader is struck by how the patient is ignored in favor of their disease. A cure must be found or a treatment sought for the disorder but how exactly does this help the patient? The twins are living a happy and contented life together but someone decides they should be separated. Why? JosÃ© has a gift that could be put to good use for himself and others but Sacks does not tell the reader whether or not steps are taken to accomplish this. The overall theme of this book, or at least the impression that strikes the reader repeatedly, is that these "patients" are first and foremost people and they deserve the same respect as "normal" people.

Important People

Dr. Oliver Sacks

Dr. Oliver Sacks is the author of the book and also a character in all of the stories. Although he is a character, Sacks is not the main character. Sacks, a neurologist, is only the medium through which the other characters are able to come alive for the reader. It is through Sacks' unique blend of clinician and humanitarian that many of the characters in the book become more than just patients.

Dr. Sacks works in a variety of clinical settings and encounters numerous patients who each touch his life in a different way. In the book there are very few stories from which the reader gets the sense that the patient is viewed as just "another patient." Instead Sacks takes personal interest in his clients and often seeks to pull out the more personal side of their story. Indeed, this is his entire purpose in writing the book. He does not seek to promote himself as an outstanding clinician but rather desires to present his patients to the reader in a more personal light so the reader can become familiar with each character as a flesh and blood person and not just another case study. For the most part, Sacks is successful in this endeavor.

It is difficult to say that Sacks develops as a character throughout the course of the book. Each story is presented as a separate tale and they are often related out of chronological order. Since Sacks is not the intended focus of the book this is not a problem and the reader is able to focus more intently upon the patients themselves.

Dr. P.

Dr. P. is a successful musician and teacher. He has a great love of music and the arts in general. Dr. P. develops a disorder which evolves gradually until he is unable to recognize objects for what they are. He sees pieces of an object or person but cannot visualize the object as a whole entity. In this way he is still able to recognize people if they have a salient feature, such as a large nose, exceptional height, or a distinct voice. However, he often sees objects without recognition. In one instance he tries to put on his hat, which is actually his wife's head. Dr. Sacks is unable, in his brief time with Dr. P., to formulate a concrete reason for the disorder but encourages Dr. P. to continue working with his music. Dr. P. learns to adapt his life to function with the aid of music. He sings songs to put his clothes on or to eat by. Dr. P. is able to continue teaching, painting, and enjoying music until his dying day.

Jimmie G.

Jimmie G. is a man in his mid-forties when Dr. Sacks first meets him. Time stands still for Jimmie and he has no recollection of events that have happened since 1945. The condition seems to frustrate Dr. Sacks and his medical staff more than Jimmie. Jimmie maintains a sense of humor when confronted with things that took place after 1945 and is still able to recognize his brother, even though he marvels at the way his brother has aged so quickly. Jimmie finds contentment and peace in the hospital chapel but no suitable treatment to bring Jimmie out of the past is ever found.

Christina

Christina is a working mother in her late twenties when she goes in for routine gallbladder surgery and ends up losing all sense of her own body. Christina is no longer able to make her body work properly and she feels "disembodied" or "pithed." However, Christina is strong and a fighter. She works hard to learn to visualize her body moving and working as it should. Utilizing this technique she is able to return home and work out of her house. Her efforts are exhausting and she will never lead a completely normal life again, but she is at least able to be home and to care for her children.

Madeleine J.

Madeleine J. is a delightful patient in her sixties. She has been taken care of by others since her earliest childhood because she does not have use of her hands. When she arrives in the hospital she tells Sacks she does not even recognize that she has hands. In Madeleine's eyes, her hands are just useless lumps. However, when Dr. Sacks prompts the nursing staff to leave Madeleine's food just out of reach, Madeleine eventually manages to grasp a bagel. Once she achieves this milestone, there is no stopping Madeleine's newfound use of her hands.

Mr. MacGregor

Mr. MacGregor is perhaps one of the most interesting and funny characters of the book. He suffers from Parkinson's disease which has progressed to causing him to walk with a significant tilt. Mr. MacGregor himself is not aware of the problem but is bothered by the stream of comments friends make about his lopsided stance. Mr. MacGregor's mental faculties are undegraded by his disease and he is able to be proactive in his own treatment. As a result, Mr. MacGregor fashions a pair of spectacles with a level attached to them in order to keep track of his lilting.

Witty Ticcy Ray

Witty Ticcy Ray is also a fun character. He suffers from Tourrette's Syndrome which has had positive and negative effects on his personal life. He performs as a jazz drummer and is widely popular for his outrageous outbursts on the drums, but he is prone to verbal outbursts that make his relationship with his wife difficult. Together with Dr. Sacks, Ray is able to formulate a treatment plan that allows him to engage in the best of both worlds. Medication tones down his outbursts during the work week so that he can function in society but he decreases his medication on the weekends in order to continue his success as a jazz drummer.

William Thompson

Mr. Thompson once ran his own delicatessen and he sometimes still thinks he is working there. William suffers from severe Korsakov's disease and must continually invent stories about himself in order to feel he has a history. William even managed to leave the hospital and take a cab ride while convincing the driver he was a reverend. Unlike Jimmie G., who is able to accept news of the present, William becomes upset when confronted with reality. He is much happier living in his own invented worlds and does not appear to feel there is a "problem" with his life.

Bhagawhandi

Bhagawhandi's story is one of the most heartbreaking and beautiful of the book. Bhagawhandi is a young Indian girl dying of a brain tumor. The tumor was removed during her early childhood but has returned in her late teens and now the prognosis is not good. Bhagawhandi accepts her fate and seems almost at peace with it as she "suffers" from visions of her beloved India. Unable to physically return to her homeland before her death, Bhagawhandi's visions transport her back to her childhood and back to India as she slowly slips away.

Hughlings Jackson

Hughlings Jackson is not an actual character in the book. Instead Sacks continually references Jackson's research. Jackson was a neurologist in the early to mid 1900s who produced a large volume of research regarding various mental and physiological disorders. Jackson's major area of focus was causes and treatment for epilepsy.

Stephen D.

Stephen D. is a young medical student who dreams he is a dog. Not only does he dream that he is a dog but, upon waking, he retains a dog's acute sense of smell. For several weeks Stephen is able to smell things on a dog's level, a situation he finds intriguing and actually misses once it resolves itself. The reader is entertained by this story but also a little concerned, as Stephen engages in illicit drug use and still manages to become a successful internist.

A. R. Luria

A. R. Luria was a prominent neuropsychologist and author of the book, The Mind of Mnemonist. Like Hughlings Jackson, Luria is not an actual character in the book. Sacks references Luria's work repeatedly and often mentions that the two corresponded frequently. Luria conducted studies of twins and multiples and also worked extensively on aphasia research.

Rebecca

Rebecca is a young woman who has been in the care of family members all her life. She is brought to the institution where Sacks works when her grandmother can no longer care for her. Rebecca is considered simple-minded and functions with the capacity of a young child. However, Rebecca has an exceptional mind for literature and theatre. She can perform so skillfully that one does not even realize she suffers from any mental defect. When her Grandmother passes away Rebecca, although heartbroken, maneuvers through the grief process in a most astute manner. She talks in bits of poetry that remind Sacks of

Ecclesiastes in the Bible. When enrolled in several classes at the hospital, Rebecca is able to articulate her dislike of the classes and ask to be placed in something more to her liking.

Martin

Martin, like Rebecca, is also considered simple-minded. However, he has an exceptional ability to remember musical arrangements and to recall the entire set of Grove's encyclopedias which his father read to him as a child. Martin exalts in music and when he is removed from musical activities he becomes ornery. Once restored to his musical endeavors, Martin is able to function "normally" and enjoy his life again.

The Twins

The twins, John and Michael, have been in and out of institutions all their lives. They have also been set up as a type of sideshow on radio and television because of their extraordinary ability to tell the precise day of the week a specific date will fall on--even if that date is 80,000 years in the future. Sadly, John and Michael are separated by well meaning doctors. Although the twins are able to hold jobs and live apart from one another, they loose their unique numerical ability.

José

José is an autistic man who has the ability to render unique drawings. A watch becomes something more than a simple pocket watch when José draws it. José is thought of as an idiot by the hospital staff but Sacks takes time to work with the young man and engage his artistic ability. José eventually begins to speak and even his drawings become more profound as if he is trying to communicate through his art.

Objects/Places

Proprioception*appears in* non-fiction

Discovered in the 1890s by Sherrington, proprioception is regarded as a hidden or "sixth" sense. Proprioception monitors the movable parts of our body--muscles, limbs, tendons, joints--in an unconscious way. People are usually not aware of proprioception until they loose a limb and experience phantom pain or sensations.

Retrograde Amnesia*appears in* non-fiction

This type of amnesia basically erases a part, small or large, of a person's life. In the case of Jimmie G., he is unable to remember anything that happened after 1945. He lives in a world that does not include anything that happened after this point in time and he is startled when confronted by evidence that time has passed. In other cases the patient may only loose sections of time, perhaps a few years or only months that they can no longer recall.

Pithed*appears in* non-fiction

Pithed is the term used by Christina, the Disembodied Lady (Chapter 3), to describe her loss of proprioception. She likens herself to a frog that has had its insides scooped out in preparation for consumption and announces she is the "first pithed human being."

Athetosis*appears in* non-fiction

Athetosis is the involuntary movement of hands, fingers, toes, and/or feet. In many cases the condition is caused by a brain lesion.

Phantom*appears in* non-fiction

The word "phantom" takes on a completely different meaning when used by neurologists. In the clinical world, a phantom "is a persistent image or memory of part of the body." In most case a patient has phantom pain or sensations following the loss or removal of a body part.

Parkinsonism*appears in* non-fiction

In this condition the synthesis of the labyrinthine, the proprioceptive, and the visual is impaired. Parkinsonism, or Parkinson's disease, is a nervous disorder recognized by trembling limbs and muscular rigidity. At present there is no cure for Parkinsonism.

Tourette's Syndrome*appears in* non-fiction

Tourette's Syndrome is characterized by an abundance of nervous energy which can produce a series of strange motions including tics, jerks, mannerisms, grimaces, noises, curses, imitations and compulsions.

L-Dopa*appears in* non-fiction

L-Dopa is a drug which acts as a precursor of the transmitter dopamine.

Dopamine is often lacking in patients who suffer from a "sleepy state." Dopamine works to transmit nerve impulses and so L-Dopa is administered as a means of "activating" the latent dopamine.

Korsakov's*appears in* **non-fiction**

Korsakov's syndrome is named for Sergei Korsakov who discovered the disorder. The disease is characterized by a lack of thiamine in the body and results in a degenerative brain disorder. Patients often loose their memories and will sometimes make up new memories to replace those lost.

Eidetic Memory*appears in* **non-fiction**

Someone with an eidetic memory is able to recall details with amazing accuracy and vividness. Martin is the best example of this in the book. He is a "walking Grove" because he can recall the entire nine volume encyclopedia on music even though he only heard it read aloud by his father.

Transports*appears in* **non-fiction**

A transport is the name Sacks gives to reminiscence. These types of remembrances "transport" the patient to another place and/or time.

Themes

Forgetting the Self

Sacks states in his preface that he desires to present the reader with a series of stories, not case studies. By depicting the lives of his patients in story form, Sacks brings back an important element many mental patients are stripped of: the self. The reader must question who or what robs the mental patient of the self. Is it the disease or the medical world which professes to want to help these individuals?

Any student of psychology, or any branch of medicine, will be exposed to countless case studies and reports on experimental groups. The student reads this information hoping to increase his own knowledge and learn all he can to help those in need. However, case studies and reports do not mention people as people. People are reduced to statistics, numbers grouped together according to common symptoms, treatment plans, or outcomes. There is no individuality allowed in such scientific writing. The self is purposely left out of such reports because any personal identification may cloud a practioner's judgment. Doctors must remain neutral and unattached when treating a patient.

This precisely seems to be the problem in medicine. A patient goes to his doctor with a series of symptoms. Those symptoms closely match a series of reported symptoms associated with a particular disease so the doctor tells his patient that this is what he has and this is how to treat it. What the doctor often does not bother to take into consideration is this particular patient's lifestyle or personality or any other defining characteristic which makes the patient unique. The doctor fails to consider that each patient is different and will react differently to the same disease. The doctor forgets there is a self involved and the self is what needs treating, not the disease.

Legal Matters

Mental health and the judicial system often overlap and cause controversy. There have been innumerable cases where a potential criminal was able to escape a guilty verdict or received a reduced sentence because he pleaded insanity. There are no clear answers to the questions which arise in criminal cases where mental health is an issue and so it will remain an enduring debate.

Sacks present the story of Donald who killed his girlfriend while high on PCP. It was a known fact he committed the murder and that he had taken the drugs, but he was not convicted in a regular court trial. Instead, Donald was sentenced to time in an institution for the criminally insane because he had amnesia and could not recall the event in question. The reader immediately thinks of a court case they may have seen or heard of with similar circumstances. In most cases the question the reader has is: is this person really insane or are they faking it to get out of jail time? The same question is raised with Donald. Donald's situation is further compounded by his drug use. Surely he should have to serve some sort of sentence for that at least?

Sacks does not seem to take a clear side in this matter, although the reader is likely to believe Sacks in favor of the mental institution over jail. Donald eventually does remember the murder of his girlfriend but still receives no punishment. Instead, he is able remain in the institution because he is still considered mentally ill but there he enjoys a life of leisurely gardening. One could argue that Donald is serving a sentence for his crime; a sentence with apparently no end in sight. However, one could also say that Donald gets off fairly easy. Instead of being forced to endure a life sentence in jail or the death penalty, he is able to live fairly comfortably in the hospital. The reader wonders what the girlfriend's family thinks of Donald's "punishment." This chapter is really the only of its kind in the entire book but it raises a very controversial issue and yet provides no more clarity or insight into the problem.

Abnormal or Not?

One of the themes that emerges is the possibility that Sacks' patients are not truly "sick." Often the reader gets the impression that the so-called "affliction" from which the patient suffers has actually enhanced the person's life. Quite possibly the disease enables the patient to live a fuller life and do things he or she may not have done otherwise.

Mr. MacGregor uses his disability to invent a set of eyeglasses that help not only himself but several other patients with balance problems. Witty Ticcy Ray actually enjoys his Tourette's syndrome at times because he is able to make people laugh with his quick wit and his physical outbursts improve his drum playing ability. Mrs. O'C. does not want her musical convulsions to go away because they have reconnected her to a time in her past that she thought was lost. Not every story has a positive outcome, but for those few who seem to derive some pleasure instead of pain from their syndromes, the reader may wonder if they are really suffering.

Medicine often looks at disorders or diseases as negative elements in a person's life. Doctors seek to cure patients based on the assumption that the disease must be causing the person discomfort. Sacks seems to be pointing out that not all patients feel encumbered by their particular affliction. Many just want to know what is happening to them--to have a name for their situation. The reader may also think of persons with savant stage autism. While these people often cannot function "normally" in society, they are often brilliant mathematicians or historians that contribute a great deal of knowledge to society. Sacks' stories force the reader to reconsider definitions of "normalcy" and "healthy." What is "sick" for one person may indeed be "healthy" for another.

Style

Perspective

The book is told from Oliver Sacks's perspective as clinician but he is also a humanitarian seeking to depict his patients as more than just case studies. Sacks tells the stories of his patients in an attempt to bring a human element to the world of neurological disorders. Instead of presenting a series of clinical case studies, Sacks endeavors to present the stories of people living and coping with unusual mental afflictions. The idea behind the presentation of the book is admirable and entices the reader, who is promised a series of stories that will both delight and inform him on a relatively obscure topic.

Almost every story presents the reality of the patient's situation. The reader can understand what the patient suffers from and how the disorder has affected his or her life. In many cases the reader can also understand Sacks' frustration at his inability to better serve his patients. Sacks presents questions, throughout each story, which have crossed his own mind while working with clients. The reader also considers these open-ended questions and may formulate several of their own questions. The way Sacks presents the personal lives of his patients allows the reader to carefully consider his own life currently free from disease and to wonder about the impact of mental disorders on people who have usually lead normal productive lives.

While Sacks' book goes far to show the personal side of psychiatric patients lives, he falls a little short of his intended goal. The reader often becomes confused and frustrated when lost in medical terminology and obscure references to philosophers. In these instances Sacks looses the reader and risks his audience abandoning the book all together. For those readers who push on, either taking the time to look up terms elsewhere or just forging ahead regardless of complete understanding, Sacks offers a reward--the next story and a new person to get to know.

Tone

The tone of the book is mostly objective but the author attempts, and succeeds in places, to present his topics subjectively. Because of Dr. Sacks's medical background, it is not possible for him to completely discard his tendency to speak in clinical terms. The introduction to each section of the book is full of medical terminology and large words which may frustrate the uninitiated reader. The use of clinical jargon is particularly frustrating to the reader who expects, after reading Sacks' preface, that the good doctor is going to do all he can to present a lay-friendly, anecdotal book.

While most of the "stories" are replete with medical terms not readily explained and contain many references to the work of other doctors' not easily identified, Sacks' does regularly remove his white coat and tell the story of a man or woman trying to cope with an unusual condition. In these moments, the reader relaxes and identifies with the person, instead of trying to understand the neurology and physiology of their affliction. These stories are the most enjoyable for the reader and actually enable the reader to gain some understanding of what the disorder is. When Sacks relies heavily on citing the work of other psychologists and discussing the patient in multi-syllabic words, the reader becomes lost and confused trying to decipher what Sacks is saying.

Overall, Sacks presents a good mix of medical jargon and prose. The average reader can still find an appreciation for the people Sacks presents, even if he does not fully comprehend all the terminology. Medical or psychology students can also utilize the book as a less intense textbook which provides excellent case studies and poses important questions to their field.

Structure

The book consists of twenty-four chapters divided into four parts. Each part focuses on a particular aspect of mental health. Part one is entitled Losses, part two is called Excesses, the third part is about Transports, and the fourth part takes up the subject of The World of the Simple. Each part is prefaced by an introduction explaining the category of mental disorder discussed in that section.

The chapters in each section do not flow together chronologically. Each chapter could be read as a separate story and in no particular order. The stories themselves are individual and exclusive of each other. However, the author does a good job of building upon the clinical information presented in each chapter so that the reader gains a more complete picture of the disorder after reading several cases. The author also ties together each section by referring back, with ample reminders, to previous stories.

Quotes

"'No, it is not. That is your foot. There is your shoe.'" "'Ah! I thought that was my foot.'" Chapter 1, p. 10.

"'You don't enjoy life,' I repeated, hesitating somewhat. 'How then do you feel about life?'" "'I can't say that I feel anything at all.'" "'You feel alive though?'" "'Feel alive? Not really. I haven't felt alive for a very long time.'" Chapter 2, p. 36.

"Clearly Jimmie found himself, found continuity and reality, in the absoluteness of spiritual attention and act. The Sisters were right--he did find his soul here." Chapter 2, p. 38.

"'Suppose you could take away the tics,' he said. 'What would be left? I consist of tics--there is nothing else.' He said he could not imagine life without Tourette's, nor was sure he would care for it." Chapter 10, p. 98.

"We are in strange waters here, where all the usual considerations may be reversed--where illness may be wellness, and normality illness, where excitement may be either bondage or release, and where reality may lie in ebriety, not sobriety." Chapter 11, p. 107.

"Our efforts to 're-connect' William all fail--even increase his confabulatory pressure. But when we abdicate our efforts, and let him be, he sometimes wanders out into the quiet and undemanding garden which surrounds the Home, and there, in its quietness, he recovers his own quiet." Chapter 12, p. 115.

"Thus, for Hume, personal identity is a fiction--we do not exist, we are but a consecution of sensations, or perceptions." Chapter 14, p. 124.

"...'I am dying,' she answered. 'I am going home I am back where I came from - you might call it my return.'" Chapter 17, pg. 155

"Vivid dream one night, dreamt he was a dog, in a world unimaginably rich and significant in smells." Chapter 18, p. 156.

"'I'm glad to be back,' he said, 'but it's a tremendous loss, too. I see now what we give up in being civilized and human. We need the other - the "primitive" - as well.'" Chapter 18, pp. 157-158.

"We paid far too much attention to the defects of our patients, as Rebecca was the first to tell me, and far too little to what was intact or preserved." Chapter 21, p. 183

"Martin did, indeed, have 'freak' musical abilities--but they were only freak-like if removed from their right and natural context." Chapter 22, p. 191.

"In the case of the twins, of course, it was not just a 'faculty', but the personal and emotional centre of their lives. And now they are separated, now it is gone, there is no longer any sense or centre to their lives." Chapter 23, p. 210.

"But the salient and exciting and most significant transformation was this: that Jose had changed winter into spring." Chapter 24, p. 225.

Topics for Discussion

In many of Oliver Sacks' stories, the main character is viewed as less than human. Do you think this viewpoint is a result of their particular disease or just the way the medical world views its patients?

Sacks is extremely concerned with the role of the "self" in his patients' conditions. Pick one person and discuss whether you feel they lack a "self" or if their sense of "self" is just altered by their disorder.

Play the role of doctor and try to formulate a well thought out explanation as to why Jimmie G.'s memory stops at 1945.

As the reader, do you feel Sacks is making fun of his patients by choosing to write about them or is his book a useful tool in the study of neuropsychological disorders?

Should patients with "phantoms" be diagnosed as having a mental disorder or are phantom limbs and pains just the natural physical result of losing limbs and suffering immense pain?

Discuss some alternative therapies which could be useful to the medical and psychological fields. For example: music therapy, art therapy, spiritual therapy.

How do you feel about Oliver Sacks's writing style? Discuss ways he could make the stories and information easier to understand or defend his use of medical terminology and philosophical references.